Barn Again

Restored and New for the Twenty-first Century

E. Ashley Rooney

Acknowledgments

This book is a sequel to my 2004 *Old Barns – New Homes: Showcase of Architectural Conversions*. The time has come to revisit barn conversions: perhaps because there has been so much feedback about the first book and so many barns have been restored, I am told, because of that book. Much to my delight, I find that many more people are into restoring, refitting, and renovating old barns. Barn conversions are not just a sometime thing, but they are taking place more frequently throughout the United States as people realize the massive beauty of these cultural artifacts.

I found that the images by Whitney Gay and Jeffrey Read also inspired me as I began the work.

Other Schiffer Books By The Author:
Old Barns - New Homes: A Showcase of Architectural Conversions, ISBN: 0764321323, $34.95

Other Schiffer Books on Related Subjects:
Living Barns: How to Find and Restore a Barn of Your Own, Ernest Burden, ISBN: 0764324101, $39.95
Yesterday's Structures: Today's Homes, Lucy D. Rosenfeld, ISBN: 0764310143, $39.95

Covers and book designed by: Bruce Waters
Type set in Americana XBd BT/Humanist 521 BT

ISBN: 978-0-7643-3431-3
Printed in China

Image Credits: Cover: Top: *Courtesy of L. Gregory Scheer*. Lower Left: *Courtesy of Jim Titschler The School of Photography*; Lower Right: *Courtesy of Jeff Read Antique Barns.net*. Title Page: *Courtesy of L. Gregory Scheer*. Back Cover & Spine: *Photo by Les Kipp*. Contents Page: *Courtesy of Jeff Read Antique Barns.net*

Schiffer Books are available at special discounts for bulk purchases for sales promotions or premiums. Special editions, including personalized covers, corporate imprints, and excerpts can be created in large quantities for special needs. For more information contact the publisher:

Published by Schiffer Publishing Ltd.
4880 Lower Valley Road
Atglen, PA 19310
Phone: (610) 593-1777; Fax: (610) 593-2002
E-mail: Info@schifferbooks.com

For the largest selection of fine reference books on this and related subjects, please visit our web site at **www.schifferbooks.com**
We are always looking for people to write books on new and related subjects. If you have an idea for a book please contact us at the above address.

This book may be purchased from the publisher.
Include $5.00 for shipping.
Please try your bookstore first.
You may write for a free catalog.

In Europe, Schiffer books are distributed by
Bushwood Books
6 Marksbury Ave.
Kew Gardens
Surrey TW9 4JF England
Phone: 44 (0) 20 8392 8585; Fax: 44 (0) 20 8392 9876
E-mail: info@bushwoodbooks.co.uk
Website: www.bushwoodbooks.co.uk

Contents

1. Barns 5

2. Residential Conversions 30

3. Commercial and Institutional Conversions 88

4. Other Uses for Barns 126

5. New Barns.. 148

6. Resources 170

Bibliography.. 174

Index.. 175

Preface

For sixty years the pine lumber barn
had held cows, horses, hay, harness, tools, junk
amid the prairie winds...
and the corn crops came and went, plows and wagon
and hands milked, hands husked and harnessed
and held the leather reins of horse teams
in dust and dog days, in late fall sleet 'til the work was done that fall.
And the barn was a witness, stood and saw it all.

From "The People, Yes," Carl Sandburg

1. Barns

For many of us, the American barn symbolizes our roots. We see that big red barn, and we visualize the smell of hay, feel the damp nuzzling nose of a calf, and pet a sleepy cat or two. Cobwebs sparkling in the light, farming tools, and bags of grain – all make up the barn in our memories. They evoke a sense of security, of closeness to the land, and community with the people who work with the land.

Attracted by the rich, fertile soil of this country, the early colonists knew the importance of barns. The New England climate dictated that their animals had to have appropriate shelter in the winter and that their feed be stored in a sound, sturdy structure. Although the early settlers built their houses slowly, they laid their barns out on the ground and raised them several days later with the help of the neighbors and friends.

Agriculture is a major industry in the United States, and the country is a net exporter of food. *Courtesy of Whitney Gay*

As Americans moved westward, so did the farms. *Courtesy of D. Peter Lund*

The top twenty American agricultural products by value, as reported by the Food and Agriculture Organization of the United Nations in 2003, are corn, cattle meat, cow's milk, chicken meat, soybeans, pig meat, wheat, cotton lint, hen's eggs, turkey meat, tomatoes, potatoes, grapes, oranges, paddy rice, apples, sorghum, lettuce, cotton seed, and sugar beets. *Courtesy of Whitney Gay*

The Generic Barn

Built on a European model, the early American barns had steeply slanted thatched roofs and horizontal siding. Doors had wooden hinges; beams were hand-hewn; and wooden pegs acted as nails. By 1830, New England farmers began to design barns that were more appropriate to their more rigorous climate. Thatch gave way to cedar shakes, barns were built higher, and the roof became less slanted.

Constructed from enormous timbers, the main frames were perpendicular to the roof ridge and, depending on the size of the barn, there were three or more. These H frames are often referred to as bents. Today, the most common form of frame building utilizes many small "sticks" (2x4's or 2x6's). Timber frames, on the other hand, are built of a fewer number of massive timbers – like 8 x 8's or 8 x 12's.

Viewed from front or back, the barn was divided into three wide areas or aisles called bays. When seen from the sides, the barn was divided into transverse bays, the number depending on the number of bents.

Barns can have several levels above the main floor. These do not necessarily have a solid floor. Instead, planks are often thrown across the transverse beams. The hay is stored in these upper levels. Large, long rafters that meet at the ridge make up the barn roof. The hayloft door nestles under the peak of the roof.

Before the 1850s, most barns had at least one pair of hinged doors or a single sliding door on double metal strips, which was generally centered in the front wall. Often, there was a similar doorway in the back wall so a wagon could pass straight through the barn instead of backing out. Later, the single sliding door on rollers became common. During the nineteenth century, gable entry barns that often had a long transom window set above the wagon doors to provide light became popular. Any other windows were placed haphazardly. Natural lighting was not considered a priority.

Since damp hay can burst spontaneously into flame, good ventilation was essential. Pigeon holes scattered about the upper sidewalls ventilated barns. To improve ventilation, farmers often added cupolas. This became known as the New England barn.

Generally, older barns are built from massive timbers assembled into a bent. A number of bents are connected using girts, which are horizontal beams that connect one bent to another bent, making a frame. A barn's structural system helps to determine the history of the building. *Courtesy of Jeff Read AntiqueBarns.net*

The hay is generally stored above the first floor. The hay is then dropped into the manger.

Timber framers use centuries-old wood joinery techniques, such as mortise-and-tenon joints, which utilize hardwood pegs, splines, or shims – not nails or screws. Here can be seen details of joints in a barn restored by Hugh Lofting Timber Framing, Inc. *Photo by Les Kipp*

Types of Barns

Immigrants brought different barn designs and construction techniques from the old country. They built barns to fit the region, the climate, the crops, and their ethnic background. The English settlers in the Northeast built "three bay barns." Germans liked gambrel roofs on their barns. Many barns reflect the local building materials: limestone in Pennsylvania, logs in the southeast.

Barns are built to fit the region, climate, and their crops. The New England barn resembles the generic barn described above. It generally has wagon doors centered on the long side, vertical board siding, and a three-bay rectangular configuration inside. The early New England barns housed livestock on the bottom floor. The floor above them stored grain and fodder on both sides of a central open area. This area in the middle was used for threshing grain, a practice that goes back to ancient Egypt. Tucked in nooks and crannies were farm implements and feed grains.

The early New England farmers designed interconnected barns to avoid trekking though the snow to the barn during the winter. The barn is attached to the house through a series of small subsidiary buildings such as a woodshed, tool house, or milk house. Thanks to this rambling design, a farmer could do a day's chores and be sheltered from the winter's storms. The resulting complex of farm buildings, known as "continuous architecture," is not a neat and tidy unit; these structures were often built at different times and with a variety of materials.

New England barns house livestock during the winter.
Courtesy of Siobhan Theriault

Barns are the places to store grain and farm equipment. *Courtesy of D. Peter Lund*

Note the vertical siding on this Massachusetts barn. *Courtesy of Robert Bicknell Photo*

Although this home has been restored, you can still see the connection between the house and the barn. *Courtesy of D. Peter Lund*

Beginning in the eighteenth century, the Dutch in New York State and some areas of New Jersey built the first great barns with extended gable roofs. Generally, their width was larger than their length. The siding was typically horizontal, the detailing simple. The massive-looking barn has a more or less square floor plan, wagon doors centered on the end or gable wall, a steeply pitched roof, and rows of rough sawn interior columns held together by large overhead anchor beams. Holes near the roofline allow the barn swallows to flit in and out.

Built in large numbers in eastern New York and New Jersey before 1850, Dutch barns served as all-purpose working farm buildings in a region dominated by grain farming. *Courtesy of Whitney Gay*

The Pennsylvania bank, or the "Sweitzer barn," is a sheltered structure built into the side of a hill, which allows two levels to be entered from the ground. Usually, the lower level houses animals, the upper levels serve as a threshing floor and storage space. The hillside entrance gives easy access to wagons bearing wheat or hay. The barn faces south, and the barnyard is on the sunny side so the livestock can be led out from the lower floor, which was dug out of the hillside. Since the floor opens to the south and is protected from the north winds by the hill, the animals are sheltered from the cold. The driveway on the north side leading up the rise to the main threshing floor on the second story is a characteristic feature of the building. These barns are often built from local, easily cut limestone.

Early German and Swiss settlers who built these barns were familiar with the forebay barns of Switzerland. In most bank barns, the main or upper part overhung the lower part on the south side by as much as 10 feet. This forebay or overshoot varies widely according to local tradition and available materials.

Farmers threw the hay down the stairway or into the straw room, where it was fed to the livestock. The threshing areas and granaries were overhead on the barn floor. These barns are noteworthy for their extensive stonework. Their thick, 18- to 30-inch walls are distinguished by a series of loopholes or gable windows providing light and ventilation.

This bank barn also has vents for ventilation. *Courtesy of Whitney Gay*

By combining one- and two-story sections in the same structure, Pennsylvania farmers utilized the gently rolling terrain, nestling their structures into a hillside. *Courtesy of Whitney Gay*

Drying tobacco. *Courtesy of Whitney Gay*

With its gabled roof, the rectangular framed tobacco barn was once ubiquitous in the American landscape. Tobacco sheds or barns were designed to dry this lucrative crop. Their venting systems, which usually require hinges that allow cladding boards to be opened, allowed drying winds to blow through the barn as the crop "cured." These barns often have rooftop ventilation.

The tobacco barn was created for a single, lucrative crop. *Courtesy of Whitney Gay*

The prairie barn, also known as the western barn, has a long, sweeping roof. Western agriculture usually involves large herds of livestock, necessitating great storage space for hay and feed. The long, wide roof furnishes shelter for the livestock and provides storage for hay and feed.

Found throughout the South and Southeast, crib barns are especially numerous in the Appalachian and Ozark Mountain states. Typically built of un-chinked logs, crib barns were sometimes covered with vertical wood siding. Hay and feed are stored under their long, wide roofs. Their roofs are usually covered with metal. These rustic barns contain one to six cribs that serve as storage for fodder or pens for livestock.

Perhaps the barn with the most mystique is the round barn. George Washington is said to have had a round barn. The Shakers built a big, round stone barn in Hancock, Massachusetts, in 1826.

The design of a round barn is based on the theory that there is more floor space and less wall space in a circle or polygon than in a rectangle. Most round barns are built with a silo in the center. The cattle are fed in stanchions built around the base of the silo, which never freezes – because it is in the center of the barn. Round barns also resist strong winds better than traditional barns because strong gusts are directed around the structure rather than directly at the walls.

America's prairies changed our way of farming. *Courtesy of Knut Wefald*

In the 1880s, as people began studying industrial efficiency, round barns became popular, particularly in the Midwest. A round barn allows many activities to go on concurrently. *Courtesy of Whitney Gay (below and opposite page)*

With the twentieth century came "modern" barns built to house specialized farming operations such as a dairy. These newer barns are easily distinguished by the use of steel or sawn lumber in place of hand hewn interior support timbers. They now have concrete floors and often have metal roofs. Their components, such as walls, doors, and even stalls, can be factory built and assembled on site. No longer does the farmer rely on holes for ventilation; fans relieve the heat, thereby increasing dairy production.

During the past century, barns have changed considerably.
Courtesy of Whitney Gay

Barns have become massive warehouses. *Courtesy of Whitney Gay*

Barn Decoration

For most American farmers, barns are generally simple, sturdy utilitarian structures. Decorative treatments are rare. When he had some money, the American farmer might paint his barn, but he did little to decorate it.

Paint

Painted barns became more common by the late nineteenth century. New England farmers produced a strong, plastic-like paint from skim milk, red iron oxide, and lime. These mundane ingredients give the American barn its noteworthy red paint. Red paint is durable, easily made, and absorbs the heat of the sun, thus adding to barn warmth. Later, farmers switched from milk to linseed oil to get better penetration.

Some exceptional farmers became quite creative in personalizing their barn.

When we think of barns, we think of them as being red. *Courtesy of Whitney Gay*

In another era, barns were the main billboards. *Courtesy of Whitney Gay*

This farmer liked a checkered silo. *Courtesy of Whitney Gay*

Some farmers really wax creative. *Courtesy of Whitney Gay*

This barn is known as the champagne barn because of the vents.
Courtesy of Whitney Gay

These vents create a vertical accent against the stone walls of this barn. *Courtesy of Whitney Gay*

Of course, the hex sign is a well-known decorative element. *Courtesy of D. Peter Lund*

The peace sign is another one.
Courtesy of D. Peter Lund

Cupola

A cupola is a small, domed structure made of wood. In the days before roof and ridge vents, a cupola was the most effective way to ventilate a stable, barn, or even a house. Most had louvered side openings to evacuate the accumulating heat. Cupolas were also a way that the farmer could decorate his barn and exercise his sense of creativity. Today, people put cupolas and weather vanes on their barns and garages as well as their homes, but many are much too small for the structure that supports them.

Cupolas. *Courtesy of D. Peter Lund and Whitney Gay*

Cupolas. *Courtesy of D. Peter Lund and Whitney Gay*

Weather Vane

A weather vane pointing in the wind can tell the farmer whether a northerly wind is bringing frost or a southerly wind is a harbinger of spring. Early American farmers were dependent upon these devices to forecast changes in the weather.

The weather vane has been around for a long time. Believing that the winds had divine powers (remember the Trojan War and the sacrifice of Iphigenia?), the Greeks made the earliest recognized weather vane in honor of the Greek god Triton. Built in 48 B.C. by Andronicus, an astronomer, the earliest vane is thought to be 4 to 8 feet long, with the head and chest of a man and the tail of a fish.

Throughout Greece and pre-Christian Rome, weather vanes depicting the gods adorned most villas. In the ninth century, the Vikings used bronze weather vanes featuring an animal or creature from Norse mythology on their ships, and they topped many Scandinavian steeples. Some ancient weather vanes are still in use in Sweden and Norway.

At Monticello, Thomas Jefferson attached his weather vane to a pointer in the ceiling of the room directly below it so he could read the direction of the wind from inside his home. In 1787, George Washington celebrated the end of the Revolutionary War by commissioning a Dove of Peace weather vane for Mount Vernon. After the Revolutionary War, the goddess of liberty and the federal eagle became fashionable subjects. By the mid-1850s, weather vane manufacturers were producing many designs in mass quantities. In the early 1900s, silhouette weather vanes, or those featuring a sport, occupation, or the ever-popular rooster were common.

The first weather vanes were sensitive, wooden instruments. *Courtesy of D. Peter Lund*

Originally, farmers used weather vanes for telling the direction of the wind. *Courtesy of D. Peter Lund*

The ubiquity of roosters on weather vanes goes back to a ninth century pope. In the ninth century, a papal decree mandated that every church show a cock on its dome or steeple as a reminder of Peter's denial of Christ (Luke 22:34) and to call worshippers to morning prayers. For centuries since, roosters have topped church steeples and cupolas, both in Europe and America. *Courtesy of D. Peter Lund*

The construction of the weather vane is the reason for its long-time success. Slightly counterweighted on one end, the opposite or unweighted end of the vane can be swayed by the lightest breeze, thus indicating the wind's direction. *Courtesy of D. Peter Lund*

Barns in Peril

Barns bring us back to our roots as Americans, as independent, hard-working people. They have a sense of harmony and balance stemming from their orientation on the land, their proportions, and their use of natural materials. They are often quite big. But this idyllic scene is changing. Barns have either become metal prefabricated warehouse behemoths, or have outlived their usefulness and fallen into disrepair. Many are being destroyed – not only by neglect, but also by the swinging wrecker's ball. Others are slowly collapsing, waiting for that final heavy snowfall or the careless match.

Fortunately, Americans, as the British have done before us, are discovering that barns can offer grand spaces, striking construction, and the imaginative play of sunlight and shadow. They have converted them for use as residences, offices, retail establishments, nonprofit centers, and the like. The key to such preservation is imagination. Their designers and developers asked the question, "What could this barn become" rather than mourning the past or calling in the bulldozer.

This massive Shaker barn located in New Lebanon, New York, measured 46 feet x 80 feet in length. It had seven bents, each with a 14-inch x 14-inch tie beam. Unfortunately, it succumbed to the bulldozers. *Courtesy of Jeff Read AntiqueBarns.net*

Today, many barns have slid into weather-beaten dilapidation. *Courtesy of D. Peter Lund*

AntiqueBarns.net /American Dream Post & Beam relocated this c. 1690 barn from Middleboro Green, Middleboro, Massachusetts—where it was the original barn for the meetinghouse—to Monroe, Connecticut. The timber stock is genuine hand-hewn chestnut. Benjamin Franklin is said to have visited the barn. Today, the barn is supported by a stone foundation and is used as a master bedroom and exercise room. *Courtesy of Jeff Read AntiqueBarns.net*

2. Residential Conversions

Barns are part of the American heritage. Many of our forefathers farmed the "fruited plain" of America, hoping for those "amber fields" of grain. The lure of a new start in a new land impelled thousands to cross the Atlantic and settle in the Midwest and West. There they built farms and cultivated thousands of fields that stretched to the horizon. Since World War II, however, agricultural practices have changed dramatically. New technologies, mechanization, increased chemical use, specialization, and government policies that favored maximizing production have led to the reduction in small or family farms. Today, we see the remnants of these old farms from the highway. Many of the neglected barns are succumbing to wind, weather, and fire and are being torn down. The demolition of these cultural artifacts not only eliminates a piece of collective memory, but also removes all the energy that had been expended upon and banked in the original structure. In short, it is exceptionally wasteful.

In recent years, as people have become more aware of preserving the environment, the conversion of barns to housing has become increasingly popular. Often, the barn is gutted, insulation added, fireplaces, windows, and other amenities inserted, and close-in parking and residential landscaping are made. Sometimes, barns are dismantled; their beams and internal structural system used in a building constructed around them. Not all conversions are faithful to the original framework, but many offer stunning possibilities.

1840 Barn

One of the partners of The Berkshire Design Group envisioned a wonderful, warm, and exciting living environment created from this early nineteenth century horse barn. Working with Coldham Hartman Architects (Amherst, Massachusetts), they had the 175-year-old post and beam structure stripped of its siding and rotated 90 degrees to allow the owners to add a lower story to the house and maximize the view of the striking countryside. *Courtesy of Gary Burnham*

The exterior presents two different faces. The western side fronting the road has a welcoming facade of intimate scale, while the eastern facade opens dramatically toward the valley below. *Courtesy of Gary Burnham*

The agricultural origins are evident from the exterior, but only upon entering do you realize the full extent of the building's previous life. The team's design aimed to retain the qualities of open space using natural, indigenous materials. The large unbroken space of the great room is defined not by walls but by the framing itself. The barn frame's horizontal beams create the illusion of a lower ceiling. *Courtesy of Gary Burnham*

There was a strong incentive to locate the main bedroom and principal living spaces in the upper level of the barn in full view and in the presence of the formidable timber framing elements. The supplementary bedrooms and the living and utility spaces are on the floor below. *Courtesy of Gary Burnham*

An open floor plan and walls of windows take advantage of the views of the nearby valley. A wrap-around deck allows an unobtrusive view of the countryside. *Courtesy of Gary Burnham*

The kitchen was designed to be the hub of the household activities. The wood support for the kitchen table is a salvaged five-sided ridge beam from the original farmhouse. The stone used for the patio, walkways, and retaining walls is schist mined from a quarry in nearby Ashfield, Massachusetts, while the countertop is the same stone in a polished finish. *Courtesy of Gary Burnham*

A countertop island defines the kitchen space from the dining area, yet allows conversations between both spaces. *Courtesy of Gary Burnham*

A wall mural of the barn's former equine inhabitants now occupies the space originally used for horse stalls. *Courtesy of Gary Burnham*

The living room allows for broad views to the countryside. Native materials are used throughout the house, including the fireplace stone and wood mantle, which is a hand hewn post salvaged from the farm's chicken coop. *Courtesy of Gary Burnham*

The planting plan emphasizes mass groupings of ornamental grasses and herbaceous perennials, creating twelve months of change in form and color. Pendulous grasses overlap and soften stone walls and walks. Taller grass species create partial enclosures and backdrops, while deciduous trees frame and soften the architecture. Ceramic containers are planted with colorful annuals and placed to accent and enhance the garden. This all-season display of textures, colors, scents, and sounds gives the garden movement and a sense of naturalism. *Courtesy of Gary Burnham*

Full Use of a Barn

Using barn wood on new stylish houses in Colorado is nothing new, but the owner of this home in northern Colorado had both style *and* historic preservation in mind. The homeowner wanted to bring some history into his custom built house while maybe even making some history of his own. He hired Sovick Design Builders to design and build a Tuscan ranch-style home for his young family at the base of the foothills outside of Fort Collins, Colorado. *Courtesy of Andrew Sovick*

The design called for four large exposed trusses to span over 30 feet across the great room. The plans also called for rustic and antique finish details throughout the home. Sovick called upon his son, Andrew, of A&A Barn Homes to find lumber that might accommodate the homeowner's dream. Andrew found a 150-year-old barn in southern Michigan. He packaged 10 x 8-inch hand-hewn oak beams over 50-feet-long and 25-feet-high, sun-worn siding, unique roof boards, and rusty tin roof panels on a flatbed semi. *Courtesy of Andrew Sovick*

After the wood was cleaned, checked, and analyzed for structure, Sovick Design Builders put their imaginations to work, incorporating all of the barn's wood into the house. Siding became soffit. Roof boards were used in gates and garage doors. *Courtesy of Andrew Sovick*

The massive beams, re-assembled into exposed trusses, inspire guests to stare up as they enter the house, much like the reaction people have in a church. Small pieces of the beams are used as exposed window and door headers; old roof boards frame interior doors and cabinet paneling. *Courtesy of Andrew Sovick*

Less than a year later, the client moved into an elegant rustic house that, despite its newness, already contained a piece of history. *Courtesy of Andrew Sovick*

Horse Barn Conversion

The clients were looking for loft living, but with all the modern day comforts: bedrooms with bathrooms en suite, walk-in closets, polished concrete floors with radiant heat, finished basement, and a heated three-car garage. Rather than build new, they converted an abandoned 150-year-old timber frame horse barn into a 7,600 square-foot dwelling. Existing granite foundation walls, built into a hill, were left untouched. Only new post-footings and basement slab were poured. *Courtesy of I-Kanda Architects*

The design by I-Kanda Architects leaves the posts and beams fully exposed, with all the interior walls weaving loosely around this existing framework. This sequence of varying spaces, light conditions, and view corridors creates zones for living, entertaining, cooking, and dining. This approach minimizes construction tolerance issues inherent in combining new with old. It also preserves the original scale and sense of openness while creating habitable spaces. *Courtesy of I-Kanda Architects*

White volumes are suspended between massive posts and beams to define spaces without fully enclosing. Tall, vertical windows pull sunlight deep into the space, while a cupola skylight illuminates the central aisle from 35 feet above. *Courtesy of I-Kanda Architects*

All private areas are contained within a pair of volumes on opposite corners of the 40 x 100-foot footprint. Each volume contains a double-height bedroom/bath on the lower level, with a lofted bedroom/bath wrapping over and around. *Courtesy of I-Kanda Architects*

Large reveals become passages for circulation, creating buffer zones for transition between public and private areas. *Courtesy of I-Kanda Architects*

Open tread stairs bring light down to illuminate circulation passageways. *Courtesy of I-Kanda Architects*

Wherever possible, the systems are consolidated for efficiency: bathrooms are either stacked or back-to-back; potable water and radiant tubes in the floors both feed off the same water heater; all ductwork for the AC system stems from a centralized interior wall. *Courtesy of I-Kanda Architects*

Lofted bedrooms on both ends have walls inclined in opposite directions, creating privacy while sharing light from the cupola skylight. *Courtesy of I-Kanda Architects*

The double-height master bedroom has a 25-foot-high cathedral ceiling. *Courtesy of I-Kanda Architects*

On the exterior, structurally insulated panels (SIPs) were hung off the original skeleton. These environmentally "green" panels arrived insulated, fully sheathed, with window/door openings pre-cut. On-site waste was minimal, and installation took a matter of days. This SIP system creates a 6-inch thick wrapper of continuous insulation, providing a remarkable ability to retain heat – even when, during the first winter, the house lost power for five days after a severe ice storm. *Courtesy of I-Kanda Architects*

Birmingham Corn Crib House

The owner of an old corncrib called Ament to request assistance in converting it into a house. The owner's father, grandfather, and the neighbors originally built the structure, using lumber harvested on the family farm and a standard "plan set" obtained from local lumberyards. Al Varney of Ament and the client met and exchanged ideas, and then the client performed much of the work himself. *Courtesy of L. Gregory Scheer*

The sun porch with its stone floor is on the south side of the house. The operable windows to the sunroom can be opened along with windows in the loft and in the cupola. The house is heated primarily by a wood-burning stove in the center of the house providing heat to the upper levels and a standard LP fired hot water heater supplying in-floor heat for the entire downstairs. The floor is over 1-foot thick concrete, which acts as a heat sink in the winter. The owner finished the floor with a paving stone to provide a finished appearance and for use during summer as a sleeping porch/breezeway type space from time to time. *Courtesy of L. Gregory Scheer*

The interior is organized around what was the central circulation space of the corncrib—basically where the tractor drove to the conveyor and the corn was loaded into the side bins or up overhead. This central space on the lower floor is where a great room is located, providing space for dining on one end and living room type space on the other. The stair to the upper levels and the wood-burning stove (at left in photo) effectively bisect the space. The windows on both ends of the house provide excellent views and a connection to the land and farm. *Courtesy of L. Gregory Scheer*

The areas on each side of the central space used to be corncribs. They had openings cut into them so to access the support spaces for the house, such as kitchen, utility, restrooms, and closets. All these support facilities are located on the north side of the house. The north exterior wall is super-insulated to ward off the prevailing winter winds and cold conditions, providing a buffer to the rest of the house. *Courtesy of L. Gregory Scheer*

The house has a strong vertical sense and high volumes on the interior, reflecting the original use of the building as a corncrib. This photo was taken from the cupola space above both loft bedrooms. In fact, each bedroom served originally as a corn bin over the central drive-through area below. The windows flood all the spaces with natural light. The effect is to be surrounded by natural light without dark corners or shadows, since light comes from the side as well as the cupola above. Both upper bedrooms look out across the surrounding farmland and meadows capturing the serenity of the setting. *Courtesy of L. Gregory Scheer*

The owner is an avid hunter and fisherman. His desire to create, to some extent, a hunting lodge for a residence is reflected in the choice of finishes. Most of the wall finishes are the refinished original wood slats. The main level flooring is an easily cleaned ceramic tile over the in-floor heat and the original concrete. *Courtesy of L. Gregory Scheer*

This view captures the relationship of the loft-type bedrooms with the solar porch below. In this view, you are actually looking down through the bedroom window (at the right) to the solar porch below, and the window outside. During the winter, this window can be opened during the day as solar gain heats up the porch and rises in the space. During the summer, the windows in the porch can be opened along with this window and the windows in the cupola providing a "chimney effect" through the house, ventilating all the spaces. *Courtesy of L. Gregory Scheer*

The entire upper loft area is lined with the original corncrib wood, which the owner sanded and sealed. The exterior walls of each bedroom were removed and replaced with windows and insulated walls with a drywall interior finish. The ladder in this view leads to the observatory in the cupola. *Courtesy of L. Gregory Scheer*

The owner reused much of the original structure, which gives a warm, inviting look to the interior. Considering the owner put in the bulk of the labor in sweat equity, his budget was really used to buy the materials and not much more. Most of his friends worked for the cookouts and beer that he supplied! The resulting green sustainable building cost the owner less than $50,000.
Courtesy of L. Gregory Scheer

Berkshire Beauty

Burr and McCallum, Architects, were asked to convert a 200-year old barn into a house for a couple with grown children and many potential grandchildren. The main barn space contains living, dining, kitchen, loft bedroom, bath, and study. An addition contains a master bedroom suite and screened porch. Two other bedrooms and a family room are located on the lower level, which is entirely new construction. A small guesthouse and a garage, also new construction, are carefully planned as an ensemble with the old barn. The siding is clear cedar over SIPs panels. *Photo by Rose Carlson*

The heavy timber beams and ladder to the hayloft help preserve the feeling of the original barn. No white or even off white wall colors were used, in order not to overpower the rich, muted tones of the old wood. *Photo by Rose Carlson*

When Burr and McCallum introduced new structure into the interior, they used black painted steel in order to clearly signify their interventions. The walls are blue board with plaster finish and original rough boards. *Photos by Rose Carlson*

The big, dark, mysterious space of the barn was very appealing. In order to preserve these qualities, the firm kept the interior as open as possible. *Photos by Rose Carlson (above and opposite top)*

All the materials, old and new, are visible in this shot of the main barn floor. The black steel stairs, the cherry floor, and the pickled beaded board work harmoniously with the old beams of the original barn.
Photo by Rose Carlson

The early evening light complements the porch's relaxed functionality. *Photo by Ann McCallum (view on porch); Photo by Rose Carlson (view from lawn)*

The cottage proportions of this outbuilding belie the fact that it is actually a two-car garage. A bay extends from the rear of the building to gain the extra length required for the cars but is not visible from the front or sides. *Photo by Rose Carlson*

The farm pond reflects the rebuilt barn in its landscape. New olive trees have been planted along the grassy path down to the pond from the house. *Photo by Rose Carlson*

Shelter Island Horse Stable

Neville Architecture worked with their client to convert a century-old barn into a 4,000 square-foot home on a two-acre property on Shelter Island. Previously, the barn was used as a horse stable with straw covering the floor and spider webs everywhere. Above each stall hung the name of the horse. The exterior of the barn was in reasonable shape, however, and initially much of the original shingles were kept, as was the original roof.

The massing of the barn has remained unaltered, but the family wanted as much usable space as possible in order to have a home that could accommodate large family gatherings. Instead of changing the roofline, skylights were added to the main structure's roof, flooding light into the vast second floor. The west facade was kept intact, the original sliding door was re-stored, and a new, more user-friendly front door added. Certain existing elements such as the concrete ramp leading up the large sliding front door, remain as useful now as it did when the horses were led out. *Courtesy of Naomi Neville*

The north facade was also largely left intact, maintaining its rustic look. The original window placement is left untouched. *Courtesy of Naomi Neville*

On the south facade, the small, square windows were moved around. French doors were added to bring in the southern light. On the second floor, the large existing doors were also converted to French doors, and a deck added. *Courtesy of Naomi Neville*

The existing square windows were all salvaged and reused. The original structure was left largely intact, with the addition of large steel I beams spanning the length of the living room to carry the weight of the second floor and allowing for the removal of the smaller horse stall walls. The beams were intentionally left outside through the winter to give them a weathered look before installation. *Courtesy of Naomi Neville*

Much of the original milled wood paneling found throughout the barn became the interior finish walls of the family room. According to the contractor, most of the milled wood had to be dismantled to remove hay, which had lodged within the walls, and to enable the installation of wiring and insulation. Some of the distinctive paneling was used to build interior doors, and the rest of the paneling became the finished walls of the upstairs children's bedrooms. *Courtesy of Naomi Neville*

The expansive living room and dining area is 15 x 29 feet. The French doors were added to allow the space to open up directly to the south facing patio. A fireplace was added. The owner did all the interior design work. The 10-foot long farm table in the kitchen was imported from a French farm. *Courtesy of Naomi Neville*

As each phase of the project was undertaken, structural engineer John Cronin evaluated the construction impact on the existing structure. The ceiling height throughout the first floor is greater than 10 feet, allowing 8-foot doors to be installed to the bedroom and bathroom. One of the original sliding doors of the barn was re-finished and is now the door separating off the family room, which also acts as an additional guest bedroom. *Courtesy of Naomi Neville*

The master bedroom is well lit. *Courtesy of Naomi Neville*

The two original cupolas were restored, and their natural light penetrates through the second floor. One cupola lights the hallway between the kids' bedrooms; the other is the centerpiece in the master bedroom. *Courtesy of Naomi Neville*

The property was overgrown with brush and shrubs, but slowly the landscaping has been taking shape. A pool enclosure was designed to entirely mask the pool so only the landscaping is in view. *Courtesy of Naomi Neville*

The Connected Barn

In the middle of the historic district in Lexington, Massachusetts, on the road that Paul Revere rode down that famous night, stood an old, dilapidated New England farmhouse with a connected barn. The c. 1870 house was the pre-fab house of its day. Somewhat later on came the Italianate brackets and the bay windows. *Courtesy of D. Peter Lund*

In the beginning of the twenty-first century, a developer bought the run down barn from the estate, salvaging everything possible: old windows, plumbing fixtures such as the large claw foot bathtub and pedestal sink – and, of course, the barn timbers. One window even has the original glass with the initials of an important nineteenth century local resident. *Courtesy of D. Peter Lund*

The developer faced many design challenges and restrictions. One of the most severe was that the house stood in the historic district, which meant that a change in its facade was not acceptable. The neighbor owned the bay window, thanks to shaky surveying in the nineteenth century, and squirrels infested the house. Construction began with a period of deconstruction where the previous renovations were peeled back to reveal the bones of the barn. The Historic Districts Commission finally accepted some modifications, including a garage, in the facade. The owner kept the old sliding doors but added clear glass doors to bring in the light. *Courtesy of D. Peter Lund*

The stairs retain the look of yesteryear. *Courtesy of D. Peter Lund*

A modern wine cellar finds space in the old cellar. *Courtesy of D. Peter Lund*

The spacious kitchen is the heart of the house. It marries old cupboards with modern technology.
Courtesy of D. Peter Lund

From the exterior, many don't even realize that the house was once partially a barn. The original materials are found throughout the house, reminding us of the heritage of the past. *Courtesy of D. Peter Lund*

The small windows mark the old stalls. *Courtesy of D. Peter Lund*

Canted Queen Post English Barn

This three bay, "Canted Queen Post" English Barn was constructed on a farm south of Lacrosse, Wisconsin, in the early 1850s. In the twentieth century, Preservation Trades, Inc., an Illinois company specializing in barn conversions and restoration of historic buildings, purchased it. *Courtesy of Jim Titschler The School of Photography*

In 2003, Preservation Trades disassembled the structure and sold it to the current owner, who had it reconstructed adjacent to an existing small ranch house in the rural countryside west of Huntley, Illinois. Silva Architects, Ltd. of Elgin, Illinois, provided architectural and design services. *Courtesy of Jim Titschler The School of Photography*

The accurately squared, axe hewn, oak timbers still bear traces of the 150-year-old barn. Oak pegs secure mortise and tenon joints. *Courtesy of Jim Titschler The School of Photography*

The kitchen and pantry are located under the balcony and stairs. Energy-efficient hot water heat is circulated through a system of pipes imbedded in the polished, epoxy-finished concrete floor. *Courtesy of Jim Titschler The School of Photography*

A loft containing the master bedroom and bath is located behind the balcony. *Courtesy of Jim Titschler The School of Photography*

The 1,200 square-foot wrap around porch was added to provide comfortable, outdoor living space, which includes a screened outdoor kitchen and dining room. *Courtesy of Jim Titschler The School of Photography*

Gem Barn

In 2003, a client requested that American Dream Post & Beam find a 30 x 40 foot barn for her summer residence in Little Compton, Rhode Island. The firm located a side-entrance bank barn with three bays in Ontario, Canada. It was built in the mid-nineteenth century. The firm modified the roof to a shallower pitch because of the town's height restriction. The frame was erected during August 2004. Soon after, they installed stress skin panels. *Courtesy of Jeff Read Antique Barns.net (opposite and above)*

The old red barn boards are used in the interior. The old barn boards are turned inside out, to give that old barn feeling. *Courtesy of Jeff Read Antique Barns.net*

The entire home was completed in 2005. *Courtesy of Jeff Read Antique Barns.net*

Quahog Bay Farm

The clients wished to change their barn into a year round, energy-efficient home suitable for retirement. The resulting site plan developed with Taggart Construction is based on the pattern of a farm dooryard. The new barn, the screened porch, the existing house (now guest house), and the garage are organized around this courtyard. A canopy over the new front door shares the roof form of the addition and stands out as a deliberately modern composition. *Courtesy of Randolph Ashey Photography*

The space once used to capture the sun to warm early morning or early season chores is transformed into a new courtyard for herb gardens and grandchildren. A new garage is located to define the southern edge of the courtyard and separate the space for cars from the space for people. *Courtesy of Randolph Ashey Photography*

Large areas of panel and glass reflect a notion of barn proportioning while allowing the salvaging of shingles to patch in other areas. Windows outside the large-scale central element are treated as random smaller details to echo the barn history. The new addition is clad in painted clapboards as a contrast and a deliberate marker indicating what is new. *Courtesy of Randolph Ashey Photography*

As the site is organized around a courtyard, the barn is organized around a central lofted space. All the circulation paths cross this central space, evoking the barn of the past. The living room sits off the double height space and enjoys a serene view into the woods behind the barn. *Courtesy of Randolph Ashey Photography*

Jeanne Handy Designs used a simple color palette enlivened by the use of texture echoing the barn's past. Salvaged boards from the barn added texture to the ceiling and a closet at the entry. LVL beams were exposed and painted instead of being hidden by trim of wallboard. Maple Europly (FSC certified formaldehyde free plywood) kitchen cabinets and living room built in provide contrast to the other painted finishes. *Courtesy of Randolph Ashey Photography*

A first floor master suite fulfills the clients' wish for this to be a lifetime house that will accommodate multiple forms of mobility. An energy efficient compact wall hung propane boiler provides heat and hot water. Flat plate solar collectors provide a majority of the home's need for hot water. Infrastructure was put in place to accommodate the future installation of photovoltaic panels to supplement their electricity usage. New interior walls were framed to allow for more dense pack cellulose insulation and greater thermal performance. *Courtesy of Randolph Ashey Photography*

The original farmhouse, which consisted of a main house with two ells, became a guesthouse in the reorganized site. The ell nearest to the addition is transformed into a screened porch. The screened porch is a common space between the new barn house and the guesthouse. *Courtesy of Randolph Ashey Photography*

3. Commercial and Institutional Conversions

Barns catch our attention. Perhaps they remind us of more romantic times or the continuity of history. Maybe we find them soothing antidotes to the pace of modern life or perhaps they remind us of the gentle cycles of nature. Some creative developers and designers are willing to take up the challenge of reworking our architectural heritage to fit the resources and needs of the present. They see the potential that lies dormant in these old barns and are enthusiastically recycling and reusing barns for new purposes, such as B&Bs, office space, antique galleries, and even concert halls.

Interpretive Visitor Center

DLA Architects, Ltd. led the transformation of a dairy barn into an interpretive Visitor Center to inform and educate the visiting public on the geology and ecology of Illinois' only natural bog. Prior to the restoration, the original wooden barn had deteriorated, upper floors sagged, and exterior walls had spread out of plumb. The firm's design not only addressed the structural concerns but also highlighted the existing dairy barn pole structure, which was left exposed in the new construction. *Courtesy of DLA Architects, Ltd.*

Amidst prairie grasses and wild flowers, visitors ascend a gently rising walkway from the parking lot to the new facility. The Visitor Center is composed of the original dairy barn silo as well as the addition of a new sympathetic agrarian barn form. The original barn was underpinned, shored, and braced, while the grade floor was excavated and lowered to provide greater head room on the first floor. A new column, beam, and overhead truss system replaced the old interior cross-braced structure. *Courtesy of DLA Architects, Ltd.*

The existing silo remains a dominant vertical element in the composition. The silo was converted into a shaft for the new elevator, creatively providing a new use for this important design element. An exterior insulation and finish system was applied to insulate the silo for energy conservation and to provide a new weathering surface for the existing blemished and spalled exterior concrete surface. A poured concrete cylinder, it has an attractive, clean interior exposed aggregate surface. Placing the insulation on the outside of the silo left the interior surface exposed for visitors to experience as they walk into the silo and ride the glass-walled elevator cab. *Courtesy of DLA Architects, Ltd.*

A sample of the existing dairy barn pole structure illustrates traditional barn construction detailing and technology. Volo Bog is visited by increasing numbers of individuals, groups, and school class field trips from the growing urban areas nearby. *Courtesy of DLA Architects, Ltd.*

On the first floor, the plan is arranged for visitor convenience and good visual control of the entrance, stairway, and multipurpose room from the reception/information center. The large multipurpose room is used for audio-visual presentations, lectures, and "hands-on" programs. The small third floor area is devoted entirely to the HVAC system. Four air handling units serve the building, providing four separately controlled zones so that unoccupied areas can be set back to conserve energy when not in use. *Courtesy of DLA Architects, Ltd.*

Office Barn

Adjacent to the bike path in East Lexington, Massachusetts, stands a natural shingle barn with dark green trim. Once it was the Locke-Alderman farm; today, this handsome post and beam building contains an architectural firm, a modern dental office, and masseuse. *Courtesy of D. Peter Lund*

Douglas Touart, owner of Touart Design and Construction, revels in finding a project that "means resurrection rather than destruction in this tear-down world." Originally, the 1812, 40 x 50 foot bay barn had held livestock; it also had been used for an early form of package delivery once the railway came to town. Then it held various other small companies. *Courtesy of D. Peter Lund*

(above and opposite)
Touart saw that that its vast space and great exposed timbers would help turn it into striking and comfortable commercial space. For the headquarters of the architectural firm, Touart peeled back the barn to reveal its bare bones in a light-filled space covered by the soaring roof. The framing members are ordered and clearly differentiated, which visually organizes and subdivides the space. Doug salvaged barn boards, added headers and purloins for texture and support, and provided movement to the vertical trusses through the HVAC system. *Courtesy of D. Peter Lund*

The street-level floor is the stylish, totally paperless office of a dental firm. Each of the five treatment rooms has digital x-rays with large-size screens for displaying that cracked tooth. *Courtesy of D. Peter Lund*

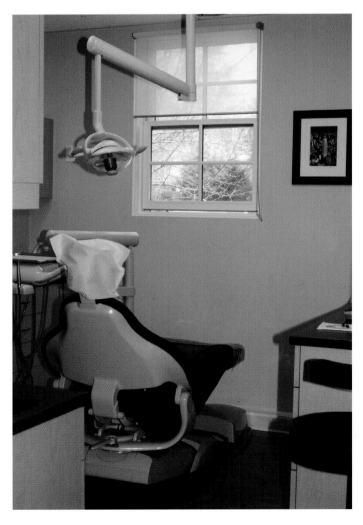

The work was extensive. Touart had to raise the old barn to replace the shingles that went down below the sidewalk. He added a new foundation that looks like it has been there forever. In the lower floor of the barn, he covered the old fieldstone foundation with new, waterproof, steel-reinforced gunite, which is molded to the several feet thick fieldstone foundation. He installed steel beams in the basement and galvanized steel pans to hold the concrete floorings and added an elevator, alarms, and a sprinkler system. *Courtesy of D. Peter Lund*

The masseuse's office is a colorful area. *Courtesy of D. Peter Lund*

An Event Center

Its unique space is suitable for casual to formal receptions, rehearsal dinners, corporate luncheons, and other private parties and events. *Courtesy of Judi Stuart*

AgriVino Event Center at Abbey Road Farm is located in the Willamette Valley in Oregon's wine country. This popular facility was remodeled from a goat barn. *Courtesy of Judi Stuart*

Amenities include a fully equipped kitchen, two ADA bathrooms, a stylish bar area, large flat-screen TV, and available outdoor grill. *Courtesy of Judi Stuart*

White Barn Project

Skip Miller of American Dreamwrights Custom Builders designed and built an energy-efficient, low-cost, live/work art studio and workshop in Stonington, Connecticut. The firm's adaptive re-use of this eighteenth century barn incorporates many salvaged building materials, including antique pumpkin pine flooring, claw-foot bathtub, vintage farm sinks, carriage house barn doors, windows, and cabinets. Energy-efficient improvements were integrated to preserve the character of the barn, include radiant floor heating, high-efficiency propane-fired boiler, indirect hot water storage tank, spray-foam insulation, and triple-glazed casement windows. *Photos by American Dreamwrights / Skip Miller*

A primary goal of the project was to perform the renovation while preserving the character of the barn. Where a lone window was once located, a door and lookout windows were added – the only change to the facade's fenestration. Exterior siding materials were replaced in-kind, with white-painted, pine novelty board on the facade and western red cedar shingles everywhere else. The original finial on top of the cupola was discovered during renovation, restored, and returned to its proper position. *Photos by American Dreamwrights / Skip Miller (above and next page)*

Railing systems were constructed of locally milled white oak (cribbing pieces left over from the structural/jacking work) and off-the-shelf cables, turnbuckles, and eyehooks. Wood and metal combine to create a rustic and industrial aesthetic and practical functionality in keeping with a working barn. *Photos by American Dreamwrights / Skip Miller*

This green kitchen incorporates sustainable green materials, including cork flooring and bamboo countertops with re-purposed items discovered during the renovation such as the wide plank bar top and butcher's block movable island (castors added). Existing post and beam structural elements juxtapose well with modern cabinets and stainless steel appliances, preserving the open layout and rustic barn charm while creating a central kitchen and living space. *Photos by American Dreamwrights / Skip Miller*

Open space with ample north-facing light makes for ideal studio and art-making conditions. Oversized, operable skylights with rain-sensing closure controls, an exhaust fan with motorized, weather-tight louvers, awning style windows, and industrial ceiling fan provide excellent natural ventilation. Salvaged cabinets, farm sink, and borrowed light find new life in this studio, while the old hay-shoot now serves as a canvas holder and the original plank floor is up to the rigors of a working art space. *Photos by American Dream-wrights / Skip Miller*

Abbey Road Farm

In 2001, owner John Stuart purchased a small family farm (less than 100 acres) to create an economically viable and sustainable assemblage of rural-oriented enterprises. The genesis of the notion stemmed from his realization that family farms were disappearing in America. His solution was to incorporate ventures that "fit in" with the agricultural landscape yet provided a means of income from more up-to-date sources. Moreover, he and his wife wanted to utilize existing structures whenever possible and create symbiotic structures on the land when they were forced to build new features. Within five years, the bulk of the Abbey Road facilities were in operation and contributing to the preservation of the Abbey Road Farm. More than 200 wineries are within a half hour's drive time from the farm, which is set amidst some of the most spectacular scenery imaginable in Willamette Valley. *Courtesy of Judi Stuart*

The existing grain bins were a unique architectural opportunity. The Stuarts located a third for symmetry, and in January 2004 began to convert the bins into a unique B&B. *Courtesy of Judi Stuart*

The wood for the three staircases in the silo suites was taken from trees on the property that were dead or dying. The treads are black walnut, and risers are white oak. *Courtesy of Judi Stuart*

To create an ultra comfortable interior space, they used radiant floor heating powered by a 50-gallon hot water heater. They also installed two 75-gallon water heaters to insure that there is plenty of potable hot water. *Courtesy of Judi Stuart*

Each of the five "country contemporary" guest rooms is 456 square feet. *Courtesy of Judi Stuart*

All rooms have a Jacuzzi spa tub and a separate shower in each en suite bathroom. Towel warmers, king-sized beds with Temperpedic toppers, Egyptian cotton bed linens, and stereo systems add to the unexpected level of luxury in these oversized suites. *Courtesy of Judi Stuart*

Canna Country Inn

This expertly converted 1840s Sweitzer Barn combines nineteenth century stone and wood with modern interior space, creating a simple, relaxing environment of style and charm. *Courtesy of Susan Ruffin*

This multipurpose barn housed livestock in the lower level, while the upper floors stored hay and straw and accommodated the threshing of feed grains. The forebay, or "overshoot," is the second floor extension that projects over the front stable wall for a distance varying from 4 feet to 20 plus feet. *Courtesy of Susan Ruffin*

In the early eighteenth century, a large two-level barn became popular in southeastern Pennsylvania. *Courtesy of Susan Ruffin*

In 1985, the massive eighteenth century barn was converted to the large comfortable Canna Country Inn.
Courtesy of Susan Ruffin

The stalls have become rooms with private baths enclosed by the 18-inch stone walls and supported by the same beams that have served as the frame of the barn for over 150 years. The forebay is a large bay picture window filled with plush pillows that invite guests to sit and relax for hours on end. *Courtesy of Susan Ruffin (above and opposite page)*

Inn at Montchanin

The Inn at Montchanin Village, located in Montchanin, Delaware, is a restored nineteenth century hamlet. Once part of the Winterthur estate, it was named for Alexandrine de Montchanin, grandmother of the founder of the DuPont Gunpowder Company. One of the few remaining villages of its kind, the Inn at Montchanin Village is comprised of eleven carefully restored buildings dating from 1799 to 1910. *Photo by Les Kipp*

The restored barn at the inn houses the hotel registration and reception areas and the conference center. Conceptually designed by Townsend Moore of Tickhill Studios, the original barn was dismantled and a new oak barn crafted and raised in its place. The restoration was true to the original structure, except for the addition of a dormer to draw indirect light into the building, creating a bright interior and a reduced reliance on artificial daytime lighting. The registration center for the inn is located just inside the entrance to the barn. With its soaring, white ceiling, white walls, and many windows, the area is large and welcoming for guests and conference attendees. *Photo by Les Kipp*

Hugh Lofting Timber Framing, Inc. used traditional mortise and tenon joinery and locally harvested oak to recreate the original barn. *Photo by Les Kipp*

The natural oak framing stands out against the white background of the walls and ceiling of the great room. The added gable end and dormer windows provide natural daylight to the room. *Photo by Les Kipp*

(opposite)
The great room accommodates large gatherings and acts as the centerpoint for the conference center. The barn's major purlin structure is fully exposed in the room; its starkness provides much of the interior's decoration. *Photo by Les Kipp*

Grasscreek Lodge

The Grasscreek Lodge, a modern take on the classic American farmhouse in Omaha, Georgia, is literally built around an old barn. Jack P. Jenkins designed Grasscreek Lodge in 2005. Stone and redwood trees were harvested for the exterior cladding. The main structural columns on the front entry were acquired locally and left in their natural state to enhance the aesthetics of the structure. *Courtesy of Jenkins Architecture*

The porte cochere provides covered access to the hunting lodge. The stone theme is carried over to the porte cochere with columns that anchor the northern facade. The cedar shake roof provides a rustic, yet sustainable weatherproofing while providing a touch of early American style architecture. *Courtesy of Jenkins Architecture*

The back side of the lodge overlooks Grass Creek, which leads to the Chattahoochee River. There are two porches on the south side of the lodge. One is a cooking porch where wild game is prepared, and the other porch is a screened in area for family gatherings. The redwood and stone exterior blend seamlessly with the surrounding pine grove. *Courtesy of Jenkins Architecture*

The screen porch has stone walls and floors and stained yellow pine ceilings. The doors are Spanish cedar. *Courtesy of Jenkins Architecture*

The Hunt Room is constructed from an old barn that was located on the property. The barn was measured, and each piece was numbered before being dismantled, relocated, and reassembled in the Hunt Room. The beams and columns are in the same position as they were in the original structure. The fireplace is the focal point of the Hunt Room. The mantle was crafted from a cedar tree on the property that was hand selected by the architect. *Courtesy of Jenkins Architecture*

The ceiling is stained yellow pine, and the railings on the upper balcony were salvaged from the old barn. The cathedral ceiling opens to dormer windows. *Courtesy of Jenkins Architecture*

A staging area for those staying in the house, the Gun Room provides storage for guns, fishing poles, and hunting equipment. The bench tops are yellow pine, and the floors a brick tile. *Courtesy of Jenkins Architecture*

Most of the bedrooms in Grasscreek Lodge have queen-sized beds. The heart pine beams in the ceiling were salvaged from the old barn. A cottage-style window was used for the second floor bedrooms. *Courtesy of Jenkins Architecture*

The boathouse is designed to be rustic. It was constructed using yellow pine board and batten with an old fashioned tin roof. *Courtesy of Jenkins Architecture*

New Life for the Old Barn

This beautiful 3-story, German style bank barn was relocated from Orville, Ohio, to a 160-acre farm in St. Albans, Missouri. The 66 x 44 foot frame was restored, and a stone foundation was added from recycled stone from the 1850s. The owners plan to utilize the barn to supply their restaurant, Annie Gunn's, and their specialty food store, The Smokehouse Market, with products from their Top of the Hill Farm. American Dream Post and Beam collaborated with the owners and Tuepker Bros. Construction to save this unique, American masterpiece. *Courtesy of Jane, Thom, and Liam Sehnert (above and next two pages)*

4. Other Uses for Barns

Environmentalists, historians, and others have long been interested in old barns. Homeowners have discovered that they can use barns for garages, shops, guesthouses, storage, and other uses – often at great savings over the cost of new buildings. A few examples follow:

Restored English Barn

American Dream Post & Beam dismantled an English hay threshing barn c. 1845, restored it during the winter, re-erected it in the spring of 2003, and completed it by the end of summer. Nearly 55 percent of its timbers had to be restored. Here, you can see original timber in conjunction with the newer oak timbers. *Courtesy of Jeff Read Antique Barns.net (above and opposite top photo)*

The firm replaced the left rafter plate and married another hewn beam into the existing rafter plate on the right side. On the right side, two new rafters have replaced the rotten ones. The new rafters were cut down in the owner's back land and were fashioned identically to the original rafters, using hand tools such as saws, framing chisels, and drawknives. Wide two-inch thick oak boards fastened down with traditional 4-inch cut nails replaced the flooring. *Courtesy of Jeff Read Antique Barns.net*

The final product. *Courtesy of Jeff Read Antique Barns.net (above and opposite)*

White House Farm

Also known as White House Tavern and the Dr. John McCormick House, White House Farm is located in Jefferson County, West Virginia, and listed in the National Register of Historic Places. Its barn dates back to the mid-1740s, making it, according to Wikipedia, the oldest barn in West Virginia. Originally built as a stable, it was converted to a dairy barn in the early twentieth century. A gambrel roof replaced the original gable roof; a concrete floor and feed troughs were installed; and glass-paned sash and fixed windows replaced the original louvered windows and one door. *Courtesy of Curt Mason, Summit Point, West Virginia*

In the late 1700s and early 1800s, the farm was operated as an "ordinary" (today known as a B&B), serving the carriage trade on what was one of the main roads between Frederick, Maryland, and Winchester, Virginia. *Courtesy of Curt Mason, Summit Point, West Virginia*

Today, the farm is a private residence, with a neighboring farmer leasing most of its land to raise cattle on the property. The owners use the loft for equipment storage and the lower dirt floor for storing a tractor, an antique truck, and farm implements and mowers. Occasionally, non-profit groups hold special events here, such as county barn tours, house and garden open houses, antique car shows, bicycle tour rest stops, and weddings, when the sponsors are seeking a historic setting. *Courtesy of Curt Mason, Summit Point, West Virginia*

Barn Media Room

Colonial Barn Restoration's (CBR) client had a beautiful antique home; however, they needed more space for Girl Scout meetings and entertaining. Rather than adding to their house and changing its character, they decided to renovate their two connected bank barns, which were about 30 feet x 50 feet each. One of the barns housed the owner's antique car collection and a workshop for tinkering with the cars. They turned the second barn into a great room, which met their needs. *Courtesy of D. Peter Lund*

The big hanging door to the left had the old hanging roller hardware when CBR began restoration, but it was rusty and hidden behind a trim board. They sand blasted and painted it and reinstalled it on a new track. They were able to locate a second, similar pair of doors on eBay that they used to outfit the door to the left. That door serves as a storm door over the glass French doors, sidelights, and transom. The doors let in good light, and the sliding doors block out the light when it is time to watch a movie. The owner also sized the doors large enough that he could pull in one of his antique cars in case he wanted to work on it in winter months. *Courtesy of D. Peter Lund*

The lantern shown in this picture was hanging on the barn when they started the exterior restoration. CBR took it down, sandblasted it, painted it, and rewired it. This smaller barn door is also a sliding door, but it is a pocket door, which slides inside the barn. The owner parks his commuting car in this bay so the crew rigged a garage door to it. *Courtesy of D. Peter Lund*

One of the highlights of the barn is the home theater. It features a high-end surround sound system with speakers concealed in the ceiling and a retractable screen that tucks up behind a beam when turned off. *Courtesy of D. Peter Lund*

The owner of the barn owned a beautiful antique clock, which was too tall for the low ceilings in his antique house. Therefore, it had spent five years in a packing case. With the renovation of the barn, he unpacked it, cleaned and oiled the mechanism, set it up, and, presto, it's working again! It is a perfect addition to this wall. *Courtesy of D. Peter Lund*

(opposite)
The owner did not want to go to the expense of building a chimney and did not think it would look consistent with the details of the barn. He also did not want to see a stainless steel chimney pipe from the front side of the barn. Rather than having a fake looking fireplace where the flames came up through faux logs, he installed a direct vent gas fireplace in the center of the great room, which turned out to be a great option. This modern fireplace, which is common in Europe, has the flames coming up through glass marbles that reflect the light. *Courtesy of D. Peter Lund*

There is no shortage of bookshelf space in this barn. Indirect LED lighting illuminates counters and bookshelves. *Courtesy of D. Peter Lund*

These cabinets are mainly used to store crafts and other items used in Girl Scout meetings held in the barn. The countertops are refinished threshing floor boards harvested from antique barns in Canada. *Courtesy of D. Peter Lund*

The owner works from home a couple of days a week, so CBR built him an office in the barn cellar. The door was salvaged from the barn interior. The Douglas fir floor salvaged from a nearby kitchen remodel was finished with several coats of tung oil, Icynene insulation dampens sound, so the owner can work while there is activity upstairs. *Courtesy of D. Peter Lund*

Loft Style Apartment and Shop

Monitor barns were originally intended for horses and other livestock and include a raised ceiling in the center of the building. This raised center is perfect for storage and may be accessed through built-in stairs or with a built-in ladder. *Courtesy of Jeff Read Antique Barns.net*

AntiqueBarns.net / American Dream Post & Beam relocated this monitor barn from Ontario, Canada, to Truro, Massachusetts. Built from northern pine, it contained 12-inch x 12-inch post and tie beams. To meet height restrictions, the firm had to shorten the posts. The dark brown patina on this rare monitor barn was unique. This barn is currently used as storage for a fine sailboat and woodsmith shop and a family vacation loft style apartment. *Courtesy of Jeff Read AntiqueBarns.net (above and next page)*

Monitor barn. *Courtesy of Jeff Read AntiqueBarns.net*

Rustic Cabin

Jenkins Architecture built this cabin using wood salvaged from an old barn. *Courtesy of Jenkins Architecture*

Its heart pine was used for the ceilings, walls, and floors. *Courtesy of Jenkins Architecture*

Garage

AntiqueBarns.net / American Dream Post & Beam relocated this Streetsboro, Ohio, barn c. 1856 to Bedford, New York. The barn, which had been scheduled for demolition, was built of hewn oak with a rough sawn American beech addition. *Courtesy of Jeff Read Antique Barns.net*

The firm reduced the barn's frame to the client's specification for a large two-bay garage. It sits on the client's property with an eighteenth century restored colonial home. *Courtesy of Jeff Read Antique Barns.net*

Meeting House

As part of a school project in the 1960s, Concord Academy purchased a small meetinghouse from a town in New Hampshire and moved it to the campus to use as the school chapel. As the school grew, the chapel's seating capacity was not large enough. Over the years, the school had added a balcony and a vestibule. In December of 2003, the school decided to put an addition on the chapel. Since they wanted the chapel to keep its original antique charm, they hired Colonial Barn Restoration (CBR) to add to the building's antique timber frame structure. CBR used antique hand hewn timbers that were harvested from barns in Canada to build the addition. As part of the restoration project, CBR also took the steeple and bell down and did some structural work to the area below the bell. *Courtesy of Concord Academy/D. Peter Lund*

Not only did the school build the church longer than it was originally, they also made it wider. The rear half of the chapel flares out. Reclaimed timbers that were used in the addition were stained to match the original ones. New windows were built by craftsmen who used the wavy "restoration glass" to match the original windows. *Courtesy of Concord Academy/D. Peter Lund*

Per today's fire code, the chapel needed to be upgraded to include a sprinkler system. CBR used copper for all its piping, which blends in well with the antique wood. *Courtesy of Concord Academy/D. Peter Lund*

The school hired craftsmen to build new pews for the addition. It is nearly impossible to tell which ones are old and new.
Courtesy of Concord Academy/D. Peter Lund

5. New Barns

Although many of the older barns are disappearing, firms are still designing beautiful new barns for various uses.

Barn Theatre

The design/build team of Archi+Etc (Richard B. Hawks Jr.) and Ayars & Ayars, Inc. took on the challenge of creating a new home for the Born in the Barn Players, which had resided in an old barn for over twenty years. The design had to provide a modern operational theatre as a performance venue, while maintaining a barn atmosphere. The team was able to reuse some of the old seating, equipment, props, and other memorabilia along with the outhouses! *Courtesy of Schrader Marcus Photographics*

The barn is constructed with heavy timber trusses utilizing steel gusset plates, which allowed the large center clear span for clear views. Insulated wood structural panels were utilized for the exterior wall and roof construction to provide an energy-efficient structure that allowed an economic way for fully exposed wood panel walls and ceilings for the barn. *Courtesy of Schrader Marcus Photographics*

Heavy timber trusses were also designed as part of the entry to give an initial taste for the drama inside. The cupolas were added to the fellowship entry to allow nature into this loft space while the cupola above the stage provides the code-required smoke venting system. *Courtesy of Schrader Marcus Photographics*

The new barn meets expectations, bringing the spirit of the old barn back to life while meeting all the updated requirements of a modern theatre environment (especially new life safety codes). The team's concept was to provide a formal plan layout that can still be found in many churches today. The audience experiences the performers on the altar/stage while sitting in the sanctuary and enjoying the show. The fellowship hall has a large open hayloft with the concession and restroom troughs close by. *Courtesy of Schrader Marcus Photographics*

Archi+Etc, Ayars & Ayars, and the Born in the Barn Players really wanted to show their respect for the art of performance, while letting all the songs, words, and dancing continue to be heard in the rafters even after the curtain has closed. This barn has lent itself well to both daytime and evening performances. *Courtesy of Schrader Marcus Photographics*

One-Room Guest House

Dahlin Group Architecture Planning designed this one-room guesthouse, located on a rocky slope overlooking ten acres of vineyard. *Courtesy of David Duncan Livingston*

This simple shed, with its natural colors and materials, blends into the surroundings. The cedar board and batten siding was stained to match the bark of the Manzanita trees that cover the hillside. *Courtesy of David Duncan Livingston*

Sunlight plays with the shadows on the terrace, creating patterns across the crushed granite patio and the hot tub. *Courtesy of David Duncan Livingston*

The 996 square-foot room feels more spacious because of the adjacent outdoor spaces. The mahogany paneling adds warmth, and the sand-blasted cedar above the mahogany trim is a reminder of the building's roots. *Courtesy of David Duncan Livingston*

A custom mahogany and limestone fireplace adds warmth to the seating area. The ceiling fans circulate the warm air from the high ceiling down. *Courtesy of David Duncan Livingston*

The floating wall at the rear conceals the bathroom while the credenza hides the bed. These large "furniture" pieces define the space without interrupting the open feel. *Courtesy of David Duncan Livingston*

The custom bed is on a raised mahogany floor, which defines the bed area. *Courtesy of David Duncan Livingston*

The plumbing and lighting fixtures are classic 1930s size. *Courtesy of David Duncan Livingston*

The 12-foot-wide credenza hides the platform bed from the living area and allows views to the exterior without affecting the openness of the space. *Courtesy of David Duncan Livingston*

Overflow Guests

A Cape Cod, Massachusetts, client purchased a pre-cut, pre-engineered, color-coded building kit from Country Carpenters. The 22-foot x 30-foot carriage house has a custom cupola, swing out carriage house doors, and forged hinges. *Courtesy of Country Carpenters, Inc.*

The clients designed the interior to suit their needs for a guesthouse. *Courtesy of Country Carpenters, Inc.*

The Barn at Spring Brook Farm

This classic, traditional Pennsylvania barn, designed by Archer & Buchanan Architecture, LTD., looks like it stood on the farm for hundreds of years. The client built the barn to house their non-profit organization: The Barn at Spring Brook Farm, which provides animal-assisted activities for children with disabilities at no charge. In 2008, more than 1,000 local children with disabilities came to the barn to work with the animals. *Photo by Les Kipp*

Hugh Lofting Timber Framing, Inc., used traditional mortise and tenon joinery to craft and raise the oak timber frame. *Photo by Les Kipp*

The upper level of the barn features a loft area that is used for hay storage. The gable end window provides natural light and ventilation for the space. The traditional joinery mimics the structure of a tree. *Photo by Les Kipp*

The upper level of the barn features an open, heated area for year-round use as an activity center and for its traditional use as a hayloft for animal bedding and feed. Bathed in natural light from the side and gable end windows, the unfinished oak beams and pine flooring seem to glow. *Photo by Les Kipp*

The lower level of the barn houses stalls for the horses and other farm animals that work with the children. *Photo by Les Kipp*

The stone piers and walls of the barn feature locally quarried fieldstone. The overhang protects the stall area from the weather and provides shade for the grazing animals. *Photo by Les Kipp*

Country Carpenters designed and installed a 24-foot x 20-foot one-story post and beam barn with loft to replace a garage that was demolished. The barn features stamped and graded, rough-sawn eastern white pine timbers, premium-grade kiln-dried shiplap eastern white pine siding, hand-forged hinges, and custom handcrafted windows. *Courtesy of Country Carpenters, Inc.*

The firm then converted the barn into an insulated art studio and showroom for a renowned local artist using a strap and wrap insulation method. The post and beam frame was erected and sided. Outside of the siding, rigid polystyrene foam board was applied along with air infiltration and moisture barriers and strapping. The strapping is a nailing surface for the outside layer of siding. The roof was insulated in a conventional manner using bats of fiberglass insulation between the rafter bays along with true vent and ridge and soffit vent. *Courtesy of Country Carpenters, Inc.*

All of the electrical, including wiring for surround sound, was installed between the outside wall during the strap and wrap process. The barn is heated with an antique-style Valiant cast iron gas stove. *Courtesy of Country Carpenters, Inc.*

6. Resources

Architects

A&A Barn Homes specializes in deconstructing and rebuilding barns and turning them into homes, garages, and businesses. A&A Barn Homes disassembles, delivers, and rebuilds strong and beautiful post-and-beam barn frames, transforming them into new homes or buildings. Once the barn frame is re-erected on a new site, it is ready for adaptation to the new owner's desires. Owner Andrew Sovick maintains that building a barn home is a great way to own a timber-style home that is beautiful, resilient, and environmentally responsible.
Crested Butte, Colorado
970.631.4337
andrew@aabarnhomes.com
www.aabarnhomes.com

Ament Inc. is a thirty-person engineering/architecture/surveying firm in Eastern Iowa and Northern Illinois. Its architectural work is primarily institutional and governmental, with some work in some specialty areas, such as athletic and performing arts centers, childcare, schools, and community centers. The practice does allow exploration into unique projects, depending on the owner's requirements and interests.

Allen M. Varney III, AIA is an architect with 30+ year's experience who enjoys working on unique projects to keep things interesting. Much of his practice is institutional, but there have been opportunities in the past to help clients that need assistance with their private residences.
625 32nd Avenue SW, Cedar Rapids, Iowa 52404
319.378.1401
service@ament.com
www.ament.com

American Dreamwrights Custom Builder is a full service general contracting company specializing in historic preservation and custom carpentry. Previous projects range from whole house construction to additions and expansions, to kitchens, bathrooms, decks, and porches, to structural and specialty work. It is American Dreamwrights' mission to build with integrity, employing not only the highest standards of construction but also integrating energy-efficient, sustainable, green-building techniques as well. The firm believes that this is the "right" way to build.
100 Captains Row #401, Chelsea, Massachusetts 02150
617. 851.4001
skip@americandreamwrights.com
www.americandreamwrights.com

AntiqueBarns.net/American Dream Post & Beam is a licensed and insured company located in the Upper Connecticut Valley, New Hampshire, specializing in old and new timber frame construction. It provides structural repair to historic timber framed structures and builds custom designed timber frame homes and barns using traditional joinery. Its highly skilled artisans are experts in their particular fields, trades that were once thought to be lost throughout time. Recently, the firm has expanded to preserve old Japanese minkas.
10 Indian Pond Road, Orford, New Hampshire 03777
603.218.6768
read@mysite.com
www.antiquebarns.net

Archi+Etc. and **Ayars & Ayars, Inc.** have been providing award-winning, creative, and innovative design/build solutions for clients all across the Midwest and beyond. Its team-oriented approach builds a relationship with owners that allows them to be involved in the process as much or as little as they choose. It strives to build buildings and relationships that last a lifetime.

Richard B. Hawks, Jr. is a graduate from the University of Nebraska in Lincoln, where he brought his rural upbringing to learning about building design and space. Although many of his designs are more traditional in style, they always have an added modern twist to meet the needs of his clients as well as the challenges of today.
Archi + Etc. LLC.
7021 L Street ,Omaha, Nebraska 68117
402.537.0330
rhawks@archi-etc.com
www.archi-etc.com

Ayars & Ayars, Inc.
7021 L Street, Omaha, Nebraska 68117
402.453.8600
www.ayarsayars.com

The **Berkshire Design Group, Inc.** is an award-winning landscape architectural and engineering firm. Founded in Northampton, Massachusetts, in 1984, the firm has a reputation for quality design and attention to detail.
4 Allen Place, Northampton, Massachusetts 01060
413.582.7000
www.berkshiredesign.com

Burr and McCallum Architects have brought a high standard of design to a wide variety of architecture commissions since 1982. Reflecting sensitivity toward client goals and budgets, as well as technology, art, and history, the firm's work has been recognized nationally and internationally through numerous publications, exhibitions, and awards. Its strong design abilities are complemented by its commitment to close construction supervision to ensure a true realization of the original design concept in the completed project. Burr and McCallum's clients range from colleges, towns, museums, and commercial enterprises to individuals building their own residences.
720 Main Street, Williamstown, Massachusetts 01267
413.458.2121
rose@burrandmccallum.com
www.burrandmccallum.com

Coldham and Hartman Architects is a twenty-year-old, award-winning, full service architectural practice designing residential, commercial, and institutional buildings for public, private, and non-profit entities. It elevates "green" (ecologically intelligent) design to a high order of aesthetic refinement. For it, a great building is one with a timeless aesthetic delight, which demonstrates an elegant (and often innovative) integration of building systems.
155 Pine Street, Amherst Massachusetts 01002
413.549.3616
Bruce@ColdhamAndHartman.com
www.ColdhamAndHartman.com

Tim Murphy of **Colonial Barn Restoration, Inc.** (CBR) Bolton, Massachusetts, specializes in antique buildings. The majority of CBR's work is in building restoration, antique barn conversions, and antique home remodeling. They also move buildings and sell reclaimed lumber.
508.527.0258
Tim@colonialbarn.com

Country Carpenters is a small family-owned business that started in 1974 in its founder's backyard. Everything the firm does is rooted in its love for early New England architecture and a shared vision for sustainable living. Its post and beam designs and building techniques are the same time-tested models and methods our forefathers used. It still hand-crafts its buildings and options, including windows, doors, cupolas, and hand-forged hinges. It has shipped its pre-cut building kits to thirty-seven states and to Canada, Ireland, and England.
326 Gilead Street, Hebron, Connecticut 06248
860. 228.2276
info@countrycarpenters.com
www.countrycarpenters.com

Dahlin Group Architecture Planning, Inc. is dedicated to the enhancement of community and the built environment through creative, quality, and appropriate design. Its expertise in urban design, community residential, custom homes, commercial recreational, and design visualization is the breadth of its professional services. Principal Mario Aiello is known for his small, highly detailed homes. The firm has won awards for homes and communities they have helped create throughout the country.
5865 Owens Drive, Pleasanton, California 94588
925.251.7200
info@dahlingroup.com

DLA Architects, Ltd. specializes in creating educational venues – from classrooms and laboratories to auditoriums to museums. Nationally recognized (*Building Design + Construction Magazine*) as a leader in the field of education, the firm commemorated its twenty-fifth year in 2008, ushering in the next quarter century with a name change from Dahlquist and Lutzow Architects, Ltd. to DLA Architects, Ltd. The Volo Bog Visitor Center has been recognized as a significant asset to the State of Illinois in its effort to conserve and exhibit the Volo Bog State natural area. It received the State of Illinois CDB Thomas H. Madigan Outstanding Achievement Award as well as an Excellence in Architecture Award from the Northeastern Illinois Chapter of the American Institute of Architects.
15 Salt Creek Lane, Suite 400, Hinsdale, Illinois 60521
630.230.0420
info@dla-ltd.com
www.dla-ltd.com

With over thirty-five years of experience, **Douglas Touart Design and Construction**, one of Lexington's most highly respected builders, has been building for those who invest not just in a home, but a way of living. Classic architectural styles, generous floor plans, sound construction, and quality materials are the hallmarks of his hands-on approach to home design and construction principles. Douglas not only personally designs and builds each dwelling along with his highly skilled crew; he understands the attention to detail and workmanship that is required to not only make

a house a home but also part of a community
71 Page Road, Bedford, Massachusetts 01730
781.275.7941

For thirty-five years, **Hugh Lofting Timber Framing** has incorporated advanced technology with old world craftsmanship in designing, manufacturing, and raising beautiful timber frames for residential and commercial clients throughout the United States. Since the beginning, the company has been dedicated to energy and design efficiency. Today, it has embraced the use of FSC certified timbers and glu lams, reclaimed and salvaged woods, and environmentally aware finishes and has a LEED-AP on staff. Its Topel Project was recently awarded LEED for Homes Silver, and its DANSKO Project is registered for LEED-NC with a goal of achieving gold status.
339 Lamborntown Road, West Grove, Pennsylvania 19390
610.444.5382
info@hughloftingtimberframe.com
www.hughloftingtimberframe.com

Isamu Kanda, principal of **I-Kanda Architects,** earned his M. Arch from Harvard Graduate School of Design and a B.S. in Structural Engineering from Cornell University. His work experience ranges from structural engineering, architecture, construction, to timber-frame carpentry. He has worked on infrastructural, institutional, hospitality, commercial, and residential projects with a focus on complete involvement beginning with pure concept all the way through to on-site detail fabrication.
364 Main Street, Charlestown, Massachusetts 02129
info@i-kanda.com
www.i-kanda.com

Jenkins Architecture is a full service architectural firm founded in 1998 by Architect Jack Jenkins. Specializing in high-end residences, hunting plantations, and vacation homes in the southeast United States, Jenkins Architecture has used barn parts in creative ways in many structures. The firm's approach to design involves a thorough examination of the client's personal tastes and an active collaboration with the client to bring their vision to fruition. Jenkins Architecture has designed over 500 major homes and renovations throughout Georgia, Alabama, Florida, and North Carolina.
6867 Mountainbrook Drive, Suite 101, Columbus, Georgia 31904
706.653.2070
jenkins-architecture.com

Naomi Neville is Principal of **Neville Architecture and Environmental Consulting**, which works on a variety of residential and commercial projects, remodels, and new construction. Because of the strong attention paid to the client, the design of every project reflects the eclectic nature of the clients and is not a prefab office design style. Clarity of design is achieved by using broad guiding principles of symmetry, simplicity, and historical accuracy allowing for small gestures of innovation that give each project its unique character. Neville's personal interest in environmentally friendly architecture and her training as a LEED Accredited Professional produce design solutions that can be applied to a wide variety of projects. Her background in architecture and art history allows the office to produce sensitive modern interpretations of historical styles and also historically accurate remodels and renovations.
36 Morton Avenue, Newport, Rhode Island 02840
401.846.8501
www.nevillearchitecture.com

Sovick Design Builders Designers has built energy conserving, high quality homes in northern Colorado for over thirty years.
750 Havel Avenue, Fort Collins, Colorado 80521
970.493.6381
www.sovickdesignbuilders.com

Building green since 1994, **Taggart Construction** specializes in energy-efficient, environment-friendly, and occupant-healthy buildings. It built the first LEED® Certified home in the United States and Maine's first Energy Star® rated house. Its experienced team of licensed architect, project managers, estimator, skilled carpenters, and talented woodworkers ensures their work will be beautiful, healthy, and environmentally responsible.
10 South Street, Freeport, Maine 04032
207.865.2281 x110
www.tagcon

Other Resources

Abbey Road Farm Bed and Breakfast lies in the heart of Oregon's wine country.
10501 NE Abbey Road, Carlton, Oregon 97111
503.852.6278
www.abbeyroadfarm.com

Set among the rolling hills of Yamhill County, **AgriVino Event Center** lies in the very heart of Oregon's wine country.
10501 NE Abbey Road, Carlton, Oregon 97111
503.852.6175

Canna Country Inn is a unique Bed and Breakfast located in Etters, Pennsylvania,
393 Valley Road, Etters, Pennsylvania 17319
717.938.6077
cannainn1@aol.com

Jeanne Handy Designs
189 St. John St. Portland, Maine 04102
207.773.2966
jmhandy@maine.rr.com

The Smokehouse Market and Annie Gunn's
www.smokehousemarket.com

Bibliography

Arthur, Eric and Dudley Witney. *The Barn*. Toronto, Ontario: A&W Visual Library, 1972.

Burden, Ernest. *Living Barns*. New York, New York: Bonanza Books, 1977.

Endersby, Elric, Alexander Greenwood, and David Larkin. *Barn: Preservation & Adaptation The Evolution of a Vernacular Icon*. New York, New York: Universe Publishing, 2003.

Engler, Nick. *Renovating Barns, Sheds, and Outbuildings*. Pownal, Vermont: Storey Books, 2003.

Rooney, Ashley. *Old Barns – New Homes: A Showcase Of Architectural Conversions*. Atglen, Pennsylvania: Schiffer Publishing, 2004.

Sloane, Eric. *An Age of Barns*. New York, New York: Funk & Wagnalls Publishing Company, Inc., 1967.

Index

A&A Barn Homes, 38-39, 170

Abbey Road Farm Bed and Breakfast, 98-99, 106-109, 173

Agrivino Event Center, 98-99, 106-109, 173

Ament Inc., 46-51, 170

American Dreamwrights Custom Builder, 100-105, 170

Annie Gunn's, 123, 173

AntiqueBarns.net /American Dream Post & Beam, 29, 78-81, 123-129, 138-140, 143-144, 170

Archer & Buchanan Architecture, LTD, 60

Archi+Etc., 148-151, 170

Ayars & Ayars, Inc., 148-151, 170

Barn at Spring Brook, The, 160-165

Berkshire Design Group, 30-37, 171

Burr and McCallum Architects, 52-57, 171

Canna Country Inn, 110-113, 173

Coldham and Hartman Architects, 30-37, 171

Colonial Barn Restoration, 132-137, 145-147, 171

Concord Academy, 145-147

Country Carpenters, 158-159, 166-168, 171

Dahlin Group Architecture Planning, Inc., 152-157, 171

DLA Architects, Ltd, 88-91 171

Douglas Touart Design and Construction, 92-97, 171

Hugh Lofting Timber Framing, 114-117, 160-165, 172

I-Kanda Architects, 40-45, 172

Inn at Montchanin, 114-117

Jenkins Architecture, 118-122, 141-143, 172

Jeanne Handy Designs, 85, 173

Neville Architecture and Environmental Consulting, 58-63, 172

Preservation Trades, 73

Silva Architects, Ltd, 72-77

Smokehouse Market, 123, 173

Sovick Design Builders Designers, 38-39, 172

Taggart Construction, 82-87, 172

White House Farm, 130-131